THE RICHES OF GRACE

THE RICHES OF GRACE

CARRIE PICKETT

Published in partnership between Andrew Wommack Ministries and Harrison House Publishers

Shippensburg, PA 17257

ISBN 13 TP: 978-1-6675-0437-7

ISBN 13 eBook: 978-1-6675-00438-4

For Worldwide Distribution, Printed in the U.S.A.

1 2 3 4 5 6 7 8 / 27 26 25 24 23

To Andrew Wommack. Thank you for truly teaching me the power and truth of God's grace. Thank you for not just teaching the message but also demonstrating it in your life.

Contents

1

The Unsearchable Riches of His Grace

For the law was given through Moses; grace and truth came through Jesus Christ.

John 1:17 ESV

Not long after being saved, I lived life trying to be "perfect." I wasn't looking for everyone's approval, and I wasn't trying to put myself above others. I knew I was called and thought that being "called of God" required proof. As a teenager I felt I needed to be something more to believe that I was one of God's chosen (I Peter 2:9). The church I attended never pushed a religious works or performance mentality on me. I just didn't fully grasp what was accomplished at the Cross. I knew God loved me when I got saved but perfectionism still became my master.

Your story may be different, but if you're living with a performance mentality, you are going to burn out. Living outside of God's grace is exhausting!

Over time, I learned that there's a difference between calling yourself a Christian and having a personal relationship with God. Spiritual maturity doesn't come with years of church attendance or service; it is in relationship with Jesus where we learn how to apply His grace in our lives.

The powerful truth behind grace is that it's never about us, what we've done, or what we can do to win God's love, acceptance, or favor. God so loved the world that He *gave* His Son (John 3:16). Christ proved the Father's love for us by dying in our place *while we were still sinners* (Romans 5:8). We were never good enough or able to do anything to save ourselves.

Many believers are living in an old covenant mentality when there is a new covenant—one that we inherited the moment of salvation.

Together, we're going to delve into the riches of God's grace, highlighting scriptures that demonstrate what this gift looks like. You'll learn how to get rid of that performance mentality and replace it with the revelation of all that Christ provided for you.

Grace is who God is. He looks at you today and says, "You're the one I love. Yes, **you**!" When you learn to live in His grace, every aspect of your life will be changed!

2

Love Answers the Why of Grace

In him we have redemption through his blood, the forgiveness of our trespasses, according to the riches of his grace.

Ephesians 1:7 ESV

When we fully receive what Jesus accomplished on the Cross, no further action is required on our part. No performance, no maintaining. The beauty of God's grace is that we didn't deserve it, but He decided to lavish it on us anyway.

You may be thinking: *Why would God take my punishment? Why would He forgive me and redeem my life?* His love for us is the answer. Most believers know that but don't realize the riches of God's love and grace go beyond salvation and can affect every area of our lives.

What's more, God desired to make His home within us, that we would be *strengthened* through His Spirit in our inner man according to the riches of His grace (Ephesians 3:16). We have been given the strength to counter whatever comes against us, every lie that goes against the Word of God. When we tap into His grace, we can identify the enemy's attacks and overcome them!

There is danger when grace is misapplied or misinterpreted. You might be thinking, "So then if God loves me no matter what...then I can do whatever I want!" If this thought is surfacing, it means you don't understand yet how to apply and walk in true grace. Grace changes our hearts.

Even a seasoned Christian can wrestle with grace. When I married Mike, we both were believers and had a good biblical foundation. However, it was soon discovered that our understanding of grace was coming from opposite angles. When I said God had already done everything, Mike agreed but cautioned, "But now we've got to maintain our salvation!" We went several rounds with this until Mike received the revelation of grace that I held.

Let this sink in: God's loving-kindness and righteousness have nothing to do with *you*. God's grace is just that good, that immense, and that rich.

3

Life as a Revolving Door

But when the goodness and kindness of God our Savior appeared, he saved us, not because of works done by us in righteousness, but according to his own mercy, by the washing of regeneration and renewal of the Holy Spirit, whom he poured out on us richly through Jesus Christ our Savior, so that being justified by his grace we might become heirs according to the hope of eternal life.

Titus 3:4-7 ESV

One of my tasks as a missionary in Russia was to line up individuals to preach at the Bible college. There was an instance where an individual pulled me aside and said that she couldn't preach because she committed a sin. Encouragingly I said, "*Well, let's run to the Lord and praise Him for His grace and mercy!*" My solution wouldn't suffice. She couldn't see past her sin and believed that God wouldn't bless the message or even use her for what she'd done. Discerning her heart, I questioned, "*How long do you think it will take before God will want to use you again? When you get things in order and feel better...perhaps after a week of Bible study and prayer?*" She replied in the affirmative.

A religious mindset demands that we earn a place of right standing. Where the Law extended blessings to the righteous, grace extends blessings even when we are in the depths of sin. All we must do is cry out, accept what Christ has done, and He answers with grace. This doesn't mean that we act carelessly. When we truly understand what Jesus has done and what grace provides, we don't want to sin. But when we do mess up, we can receive His forgiveness and then move forward.

The Lord knows that we are going to sin at times, but He still doesn't give us what we deserve. Rather, He already sees us as cleansed and completely new in our inner man because of Jesus.

Grace has the capacity to truly expand our perspective of God if we can get beyond ourselves. *We* are the ones who put limits on God because of our past. We limit Him by believing He cannot heal, provide, or bless us because of our sin. That means we see our sin as greater than God.

Imagine you are in a revolving door. If you look out, you see Jesus inviting you to step into grace. You can step out and access that grace, or you can walk in circles mulling over your sin. Choose to step out and experience the freedom of His grace today!

4

Reigning in Life

Therefore, as one trespass led to condemnation for all men, so one act of righteousness leads to justification ***and life*** *for all men.*

Romans 5:18 ESV

To truly understand the riches of God's grace we need to realize that the Kingdom of God came *toward* us! God made movement toward us. He sent His Son, whose perfect obedience satisfied all the requirements of the Old Covenant. Now, we freely have access to this newness of life (Acts 17:28).

Man's sinful nature couldn't be united in true fellowship with a holy God. That was the consequence of Adam's disobedience. However, because of what Jesus accomplished on the Cross, when we believe, we receive! Romans 5:17 says, *"For if, because of one man's trespass, death reigned through that one man, much more will those who receive the abundance of grace and the free gift of righteousness reign in life through the one man Jesus Christ."* (ESV).

So why do Christians struggle to receive God's blessings? They believed on Jesus for salvation. Is He not trustworthy enough for provision? For healing? Wouldn't Jesus also be the answer to a failing marriage? Why do believers look for answers outside of Christ?

Grace does not say, "After you receive salvation, go back and live under the Old Covenant Law. Perform. Work. Make sure you don't mess up or else you will not inherit anything." No. We are rightful heirs of our Father who grants us access to our inheritance, righteousness, holiness, eternal life, and the very best of help, counsel, and guidance for our everyday issues. Our inheritance is not revoked each time we miss the mark.

Jesus Christ ushered in a better covenant based on better promises (Hebrews 8:6). The indwelling of the Holy Spirit is what makes the New Covenant better. We host the Spirit of the living God! We don't need to struggle for answers to our everyday problems. All we need to do is to look within and believe that He is our ever-present help in times of trouble (Psalm 46:1).

Jesus is the Way, the Truth, and the Life (John 14:6). We have access to all that He is. When we accept Him, we have all that we need to reign in this life.

5

Grace Fortifies and Ignites Faith

I am the door. If anyone enters by me, he will be saved and will go in and out and find pasture.

John 10:9 ESV

When the prodigal son came to his senses, he was a disheveled mess enveloped in the stench of pigpen. He knew he had disqualified himself to be called a son but was ready to be called a servant if his father agreed.

His father, who had been watching and waiting, saw his son from afar and raced toward him. The father hugged and kissed him and put his best robe around him. He threw a party because his son was back where he belonged (Luke 15:11-23).

Being a servant would have suited the son, but the father wouldn't hear of it. He looked past his son's sin and appearance and gave him all the rights and privileges of a son.

This is the grace of our heavenly Father. He doesn't care that we're not cleaned up; He already knows the sinful state we've been in, how rebellious we've been. When our repentant hearts call out, *"Lord, I need You,"* God responds with compassion.

Religion is such a shallow representation of what real relationship with God is. The power of grace saves and cleanses us and sets us up to live at a level of intimacy where a true Father-child relationship thrives. The children of Israel never had that kind of bond with God. They had a form of relationship, but they didn't know Him intimately.

Jesus is the door to this relationship. Past wounds might tell you you're disqualified or barred from entry but that is a lie. God is ready to receive you, to heal and restore the most broken places of your life.

Entering through the *Door* means you'll find pasture—rest and regeneration. Your life is fortified because you've allowed grace to become your teacher.

You can live confident that He has your back in every situation.

As a child of God, you have access to all that Jesus has provided for you. Freedom is yours today. Simply knock, and the Door will be opened to you (Matthew 7:7).

6

Grace's Dominating Power

My child, listen to what I say, and treasure my commands. Tune your ears to wisdom, and concentrate on understanding. Cry out for insight, and ask for understanding. Search for them as you would silver; seek them like hidden treasures.

Proverbs 2:1-4 NLT

Becoming a student of the Word begins with treasuring it! There's a lot of ground to cover from Genesis to Revelation, but our Christian walk is exactly that—a walk. It's not a sprint, but a journey of discovery. God satisfies the thirsty and fills the hungry with good things (Psalm 107:9).

Ephesians 1:7 says, "*In Him we have redemption through His blood, the forgiveness of our trespasses,* ***according to*** *the riches of His grace.*" The words *according* *to* in the Greek translate to *kata* which means "down." This word carries the idea of *domination*. Domination speaks of *control*. We can then say **forgiveness of our trespasses was dominated, brought down, or controlled by the riches of grace.**

Riches in this same verse is translated *ploutos*, which speaks of the *wealth, abundance,* or the *plentitude* of God's grace. Essentially, sin is *controlled, brought down, and dominated* by *abundance, wealth, and plentitude* of grace. "Plentitude" is infinite in proportion. Abundance and wealth convey something that's limitless and never-ending. Therefore, sin has no mastery because it has been **dominated by limitless and never-ending grace**. That includes all sin—past, present, and future!

Many of us already understand that grace is unmerited favor. But grace is also defined as God's ability working in us, enabling us to do what we cannot do on our own.

Because we have been cleansed by Christ's blood and are in right standing with God, we have a reservoir of His power living inside of us. When we understand ALL that grace is, we can start to raise our hands and say, "Lord, nothing is impossible with You. I believe that this situation is turning around. I thank You that Your work on the cross defeated temptation, lack, and sickness! Because of your abundant ability that You have released within me, I can have peace, joy, and authority over the enemy. I am filled to overflowing and I will never run dry!"

This is the heartbeat of grace!

7

Surrender to the Truth of Grace

And the Word became flesh and dwelt among us, and we have seen his glory, glory as of the only Son from the Father, full of grace and truth.

John 1:14 ESV

We can see and know who God is through studying the life of Jesus. The Son fully knew the Father and understood that the abundance and ability of God was His to access. Jesus modeled a lifestyle of grace we can also walk in.

Many of us think things like, "Someday, when I'm spiritually mature, I will earn my breakthrough from God." But the reality is, we don't mature to get to a place of favor; we mature in our understanding of what we've already been given, who we've already become.

The enemy can hinder us by convincing us to submit to natural circumstances: "I can't do that. The doctor says it's incurable. There is always more month than there is paycheck." However, God calls us to surrender to the truth of grace because grace is more powerful than what we see in the natural. Out of the overflow of His fullness, we inherited grace heaped upon more grace (John 1:16)!

People stiff-arm this truth because they default to the natural. They agree that Jesus was 100 percent man and 100 percent God, but they look at the details of their lives and say, "I'm not Jesus."

You and I can never earn grace. It's not about us or what we can do. Grace is available to us through what Jesus did. That means we can live in this natural world while operating with God's supernatural ability just like Jesus!

John 1:1 says that Jesus was in the beginning with God. So, when we invite Jesus to be our Lord and Savior, we can truly learn the fullness of who God is and what He wants to do in and through us.

This is the great exchange. Our old, sinful life is gone! We've become new creatures with His supernatural ability. "Someday" is today!

8

The Old Versus the New

And you He made alive, who were dead in trespasses and sins, in which you once walked according to the course of this world, according to the prince of the power of the air, the spirit who now works in the sons of disobedience.

Ephesians 2:1-2 NKJV

Before we were saved, we tried to navigate life on our own, believing it would satisfy us. We tried to find our security and identity in people and worldly pleasures. Following our flesh came naturally, and we liked how sin made us feel. The prince of this world was the voice we followed.

But not anymore! Praise God that we have been made alive! We've landed on a new course, full of blessing and ability. Remaining on this new course comes by renewing our minds (Romans 12:2). Mind renewal is not a religious activity, but rather a part of the maturing process. When we don't allow ourselves to be transformed by the Word, it is possible to find ourselves veering into our former lifestyles—the old course.

The enemy would like nothing more than for us to revert to our former folly. Remaining on His course means growing in grace and understanding our inheritance. The more we grow, the more we know; and the enemy knows that knowledge gives us the advantage to influence our world.

God has made His abundant grace available to all who will receive it. He knew what He was doing. Only His redemptive work completely cleanses us and makes room for Him to live within us. Yet, we have a choice. He never forces us to choose Him. We still have free will.

Weigh the old against the new and ask yourself, "What course do I want to play on today?" The choice is yours.

9

Dead Men Don't React

Trust in the LORD with all your heart, and do not lean on your own understanding. In all your ways acknowledge him, and he will make straight your paths.

Proverbs 3:5-6 ESV

As believers, we are no longer sinners. We no longer live in daily defeat. Because of what Jesus has done, we are raised up into His glory. Because we are seated with Him high above in heavenly places, our perception of the flesh can be put into the proper perspective.

Romans 6:11 says that we must reckon ourselves dead to sin but alive in Christ. If we can walk around with that reality, nothing will move us.

When we don't take offense or become overly emotional, we are dead to sin and flesh. Insults may come and may take us by surprise, but we don't get rattled like the world would expect. The temptation to retaliate may be there, but that is not our "go-to." Rather, our first response is telling our flesh, "Nope, you are dead. I've been made alive in Christ, so I will not react that way."

When we do that, the Spirit of God who lives in us can rise and dominate any temptation. The enemy's resolve will seem to grow stronger, and he'll be waiting to accuse or condemn us if we react. But our resolve becomes just as fierce.

You can't offend a dead man. We no longer walk after sin and flesh. We acknowledge our God and He makes our paths straight. We have been made alive in Christ!

10

Conduits for Grace

For the grace of God that brings salvation has appeared to all men, teaching us that, denying ungodliness and worldly lusts, we should live soberly, righteously, and godly in the present age.

Titus 2:11-12 NKJV

When my husband Mike and I were missionaries, we encountered people whose lives were hijacked by religion. Their days were plagued by thinking they had to maintain their righteousness. When we ministered grace and stressed that it was no longer what they did but what Christ did for them, they were set free. They became lovers of the Word and yielded their hearts to the powerful covering of grace.

However, there were others who were angered, believing our message gave license to sin. They felt people would live a sinful lifestyle and then casually come to God for forgiveness. Mike and I decided that the grace message either caused revival or revolt.

Grace is a great revealer. It reveals God's heart toward us and reveals if we've chosen to access grace or to abuse it. If we've chosen the latter, we've decided to walk according to the course of this world to fulfill the desires of the flesh (Ephesians 2:2-3).

The sad truth about habitually living after the flesh is that it has the potential to harden our hearts. As ministers, we are prime targets for the enemy because our hearts and our callings are precious to God. We need to be on guard and allow grace to be our tutor so we're ready to deny sin its power and influence.

I believe we need to learn to articulate grace accurately. Anything that comes from our lips should never hint that grace gives license to sin. Rather, we need to keep growing in our own understanding of grace. We have to rely on Him to help us communicate it.

We should sense an urgency for the age we live in. This world is filled with an abundance of every evil work. We need to lay hold of God's Word and run with it like the Apostle Paul, teaching others that the gospel is the power of God for salvation for everyone who believes (Romans 1:16). Choose to pursue His grace for yourself and others today.

11

Sin Is Not Your Master

For sin shall not have dominion over you, for you are not under the law but under grace.

Romans 6:14 NKJV

If we could fully wrap our minds around the idea that the Spirit of God lives inside of us, we would not struggle with sin. His Spirit within us is the power of His grace for our lives.

Ephesians 3:16 tells us that the riches of God's grace provide strength through His Spirit who already lives in us. We don't have to fight to get it—we just tap into it! Yet many of us don't access this power; we act like the world. There's an aspect of hypocrisy in our lives when we downplay grace's power.

Grace is so much greater than forgiving sin. However, the real matter we must consider is that at the end of the day, God hates sin—every manifestation of it. That includes sickness, disobedience, depı worry, and poverty.

We also shouldn't echo what the world says is normal. "This is flu season, I'll probably get it." "My marriage won't last." "I'm at that age where aches and pains are just there." These statements may seem harmless, but they are part of the curse sin brought, and we've been delivered from sin! Any manifestation of sin doesn't have to be part of our lives.

Living life straddled with one foot in the Kingdom of God and the other in darkness is a choice. Moving back and forth keeps us from making progress. But sin loses its power when we learn to hate what God hates.

We are no longer sin's puppet; we are under grace. We don't have to struggle because we've been translated into a new realm where we can see the world for what it is and identify the enemy for who he is.

The riches of God's grace makes it possible for us to live out the Gospel of grace. This is our reality today!

12

Daily Invitation

Let us therefore come boldly unto the throne of grace, that we may obtain mercy, and find grace to help in time of need.

Hebrew 4:16 KJV

People have understood grace as God's ability to forgive sin; but that's actually mercy. God's love is like a two-sided coin—mercy and grace. Mercy forgave us of sin, but grace sets us free from the dominion of sin. Misunderstanding and immaturity say that we can sin and just run to God for forgiveness. It's true we do run to God, but we need to access grace to help keep our flesh from surrendering to sin.

In the Amplified version, Titus 2:11 says that we are to reject ungodliness and worldly desires in order to live godly lives with a purpose *that reflects spiritual maturity.* Too many people remain in a baby stage of Christianity. They love God, run to Him, and are grateful for His mercy to forgive, but that's where they stop. They don't heed the daily invitation to sit with God and let Him teach them how to separate themselves and come out of the world (2 Corinthians 6:17).

When we mature, our appetites change. My son Michael inherited my sweet tooth. For him, it's sugar, sugar, sugar! He can easily eat a piece of cake with a popsicle and gulp it down with a can of soda! Thankfully, I have outgrown my crazy desire for that much sugar. My tastes and appetite have *matured* to enjoy a healthier menu.

This is how it is when we grow and mature in the riches of God's grace. We read about the promises of God in His Word and chase after them. We will find that godly things only bring life, victory, and a revelation of who we truly are and what we've truly been given. When we taste and see how good God is, sin leaves a terrible aftertaste.

13

It's All About Choice

And what agreement has the temple of God with idols? For you are the temple of the living God.

II Corinthians 6:16a NKJV

If you have chosen to receive salvation, you are now called a son or daughter. Regardless of if you are a Jew or Gentile, regardless of if you were stuck in a form of religion or just carnality, you are now a new creation in Christ (2 Corinthians 5:17).

Some people claim that, because of grace, everyone is automatically saved and going to Heaven whether they choose it or not. If salvation was automatic, free will would not exist. There would be no difference between Christians and the world. The reality is, God Himself tells us to make a choice and be separate from the world (II Corinthians 6:17). Salvation and relationship with God happen by choice, not automatically.

When we get saved, it may look like there is still no difference between us and the world. Most of us don't see an immediate manifestation of change at the point of salvation. We may not have stopped swearing or having bad thoughts. Our tastes for the things of the world may even still be with us. However, the more we choose to stay connected to the Word and stay within the boundaries of our relationship with God, the more He can work in our lives. That's why we cannot separate our relationship with God from our relationship with the Word.

If we find that we aren't focusing on the Word and our relationship with God, we will never become who God has made us to be.

One mindset says, "It's easier to ask for forgiveness than to get permission." But this mindset really refers to acting out of the flesh first, then asking for God's forgiveness later. Forgiveness is amazing, but using grace's power to resist sin is where you will find true victory. Will you choose the power of His grace today?

14

Humility Is Key

Submit yourselves therefore to God. Resist the devil, and he will flee from you.

James 4:7 ESV

The only power sin has is to tempt you. When you understand the power of grace, you can resist temptation, knowing you've been crucified with Christ (Galatians 2:20). However, if you carry a casual attitude toward grace, you will cave to the temptation of sin to control your life, molding it into everything your flesh wants it to be.

When I dealt with perfectionism, I was attracted to self. I felt that I had to do everything right and be perfect for everyone. I'd go from pride to self-condemnation, then repeat. I had landed there partly because I had taken James 4:8 out of context: *Cleanse your hands, you sinners, and purify your hearts, you double-minded.* I was working to get my actions pure.

If we truly want to see transformation in our lives, humility is key. It is the first rung on the ladder that ascends to victory. James 4:6 says God opposes the proud but gives grace to the humble. Humility is running to Him and seeking His help (Hebrews 4:16). God never distances Himself. He is always there over our shoulder waiting to pour more grace on us. He knows that when we live a lifestyle apart from grace, the battle with temptation rages on. Sin aims for all targets—our flesh, our pride, our status. It will tell us how to fix our spouse and where to manipulate finances. Sin acquaints us with what failure looks like.

Humbling ourselves proves that the Spirit within us is more than able to overcome sin and live a life submitted to God—a life of victory.

15

The Stubbornness of Sin

Set your mind and keep focused habitually on the things above [the heavenly things], not on things that are on the earth [which have only temporal value].

Colossians 3:2 AMP

I want to identify five steps that I believe will help those feeling powerless against sin. If this is you, this is not meant to condemn you—but to set you free!

Number 1: Evaluate what you are focusing on. Actions follow thoughts. When you entertain ungodly thoughts, you're not setting yourself up for success. Letting your mind feed on sin gives strength to it.

Number 2: Run to God and stay there! A relationship with God brings abiding pleasure, sin only brings temporary pleasure. James 1:14 says that each person is tempted when he is lured by his own desire. Anger is passing, frustration is temporary; but, when you act on those things, it is easy to become a slave to sin. Run to the Father and He will help you keep your mind on good things.

Number 3: <u>Be realistic about the devastation of sin.</u> Sin isn't something to be casual about. James 1:15 says that after desire is conceived, it gives birth to sin, and when sin is full grown, it brings forth death. When you say something like, *"It's no big deal, everyone does it,"* it's like a careless spark that becomes a wildfire. Sin that starts off small has the potential to harden your heart.

Number four: <u>Grow in your understanding of God's character</u>. Being stuck in sin may cause you to misunderstand the character of God. The enemy tries to pervert God's nature. He will say God is a killjoy. Then he encourages you to walk in sin because God's love covers a multitude. God does forgive, but there could be damaging consequences that hurt you and those around you. Keeping your mind focused on God will protect you from wrong ideas about God's character.

Number 5: <u>Stop relying on your own ability.</u> You didn't deserve grace, and you don't have any power within yourself to victoriously walk in it. It's all Him. Trust in Jesus' righteousness and grace for you!

Again, this is not meant to condemn you, but to help you take your rightful place as God's child and resist sin! Ask the Holy Spirt to help you with each step, and you'll begin to see that sin has no power over you.

16

The Man Full of Grace

Then Jesus answered and said to them, "Most assuredly, I say to you, the Son can do nothing of Himself, but what He sees the Father do; for whatever He does, the Son also does in like manner."

John 5:19 NKJV

I love the magnificence of the Father portrayed in the life of Jesus. Jesus did not exploit His equality with God, but humbled Himself and came to live as a man (Philippians 2:6). He came as our perfect sacrifice and fulfilled the Law. Many times people will say, "Well, there you go. Jesus was God; it was easy for Him to live without sin. He was perfect and I'm not!"

Jesus had to come as a man to show us that it was possible to be full of the Spirit and fully dependent on God. He wasn't just born ready to minister: "*And the child grew and became strong, filled with wisdom. And the favor of God was upon him*" (Luke 2:40 ESV).

Jesus spent time alone to pray and be with the Father; to be taught and strengthened in the Spirit. This is a beautiful demonstration of relationship. Jesus said He could not do anything of Himself: "*When you have lifted up the Son of Man, then you will know that I am he, and that I do nothing on my own authority, but speak just as the Father taught me*" (John 8:28 ESV).

As followers of Jesus, we are called to depend upon our relationship with God. This is key if we're to live victoriously. Every success, every miracle, and every victory will come naturally when we access and apply the riches of God's grace to our lives. That's why Jesus was able to say that whoever believed on Him would do even greater works (John 14:12).

Be encouraged and strengthened. God doesn't see our limitations or our pasts. He says, "*Arise and shine for the glory of the Lord has risen upon you.*" His grace has the power to transform our lives so that we are living demonstrations of His ability, strength, and hope.

17

Everything Is Possible with God

If you had known me, you would have known my Father also. From now on you do know him and have seen him.

John 14:7 ESV

Jesus came down to our level to bring us up to His! When we accepted Christ, we were given the ability to know God's character and nature. This is why everything is possible with God—we have His Spirit living on the inside of us, empowering us, and walking with us as we transform into the image of Christ. Jesus pleased the Father (Matthew 3:17); therefore, we please the Father. He doesn't see our failures; He sees Jesus' victory.

The enemy lies and tells us that we're never going to change or rise to the level of Christ, so we feel stuck. We end up believing what we see in the natural and live our lives complaining, whining, fearing, and despairing.

In order to be set free and get "unstuck," we need to understand that the Spirit of God lives on the inside of us. He is more than enough and greater than anything we face! His grace will transform our perceptions to line up with how He sees who we are, what we have, and what we can do.

Grace is abundantly available to us; we just need to believe that. If we don't seek to understand the riches of His grace, we will have a hard time walking in faith. Why? Because we will make it about how "good" or "bad" we are doing that day instead of Jesus' finished work.

In ministering all over the world, I've seen believers trying so hard to attain a certain *level* of faith. They demonstrate their faith through working and confessing, thinking that these prompt God to move. People hear, *"You've got to have faith,"* and think that means they have to pray more, read the Bible more, memorize scripture, and then hope their faith is "strong enough" to convince God to move. If not, they need to do more of the same.

Our confessions come from believing what God has already done. Isaiah 53:5 says that we are healed by His stripes, not by our works. Faith develops from a grateful heart that understands the riches of grace. When you get a revelation of that, you will see your prayers shift—you will stop trying to convince God to move and instead thank Him for what He has already provided. That's when true faith comes!

18

Your Position and Possession

He who believes in the Son has everlasting life; and he who does not believe the Son shall not see life...

John 3:36a NKJV

We've been given the promise of everlasting life! That means life *now* and forever. We've become children of the Most High and possess the rights and privileges of a son. Our inheritance is sealed, but in our understanding, we've only scratched the surface.

God wants to show off the riches of His love in our lives. He's able to do exceedingly abundantly above all that we ask or think (Ephesians 3:20). It's time we stop seeing ourselves as a child on the edge, needing to tread on eggshells. That is not living.

In fact, our opening verse says that he who does not believe shall not see life. That's heartbreaking. When I see the world and all its wickedness, righteous indignation boils within me but also compassion. Part of grace is inheriting the heart of God. Compassion moves me because I've grown to hate what God hates; and He hates to see His creation being abused by the enemy.

People around us are looking for life; they want hope. We have the opportunity and privilege to represent God through the way we live. We've been given the absolute fullness of who God is. We don't have limited options—we have a limitless God! Because we know our position, we're fully empowered. We don't lack any gift (1 Corinthians 1:5-6). We're well-equipped to share the message of grace. And not only to the lost, but also to fellow believers who don't possess the understanding of what they already have in Christ.

The devil is on a rampage to keep people in bondage. Freely we have received so freely we give (Matthew 10:8). The message of the hour is Jesus—the way, the truth, and the life (John 14:6). The devil only comes to steal, kill and destroy, but we proclaim Jesus, that He came and paid for everyone to have life in abundance (John 10:10)!

19

Hope

Blessed be the God and Father of our Lord Jesus Christ, who has blessed us in Christ with every spiritual blessing in the heavenly places.

Ephesians 1:3 ESV

I grew up working on my family's cattle farm on the plains of Colorado. The hard work made the days seem longer and hotter than they actually were. What I would have given for a refreshing, cool wind! This is how people may feel when they've spent too long in the heat of their despair. What they would give for a refreshing turn around or do-over.

God has blessed us with every spiritual blessing (Ephesians 1:3). This is truly what grace is about. Grace looked at us and prepared our beautiful salvation even when we were in our mother's womb! He chose us before the foundation of the world so that we could stand blameless with full access as a member of God's family. This was according to the good pleasure of His will (verses 4-5). He sees us as beloved and treasured. This is what grace lavished on us; this is our inheritance. If we don't choose to receive this, we'll feel trapped believing that none of the spiritual blessings belong to us.

We aren't destined to live without hope. A refreshing, cool wind of repentance is ours to take, and a fresh perspective to see where we rightly belong. Our Father hasn't been waiting with arms crossed, rolling His eyes... He's ready to welcome us and heap grace upon grace on us!

Today is the day you turn back to God. Don't drag your feet in shame or fear but run boldly knowing that His grace is greater than any negative thing you may see in your life. Abundant life is found in intimacy.

The life that God offers you is full of hope for every circumstance; it shows you what could be: *"This may have thrown me for a loop, but this problem hasn't seen anything yet!"*

20

Grace Is Our Miracle

And do not be conformed to this world, but be transformed by the renewing of your mind, that you may prove what is that good and acceptable and perfect will of God.

Romans 12:2 NKJV

When Jesus said, *"It is finished,"* you and I gained access to the extravagance of grace. There wasn't any effort or striving on our part. We only said *yes and* received it. The beauty behind this miracle is that it is so simple; and while it is simple, grace calls us to more.

We thoroughly enjoy the promises of God, but more importantly, we have access to the fullness of God for every area of our lives. Through Him we live and minister His overwhelming goodness to others. That is why the Gospel is called the Good News.

Isaiah 60:1 tells us to arise and shine for our light has come and the glory of the Lord is risen upon us. People will see the fruit of our revelation of grace. We don't respond like the world, instead of getting discouraged or angry, we speak life. This is why Romans 12:1 tells us to present our bodies as a living sacrifice. When we humble ourselves in relationship, we receive God's counsel on how to best steward our gifts and callings.

Too many people have allowed the voice of others to mess with their inheritance. We cannot let that happen. There's a world craving to see something real, so the way we stand makes others take notice. We're no longer enticed to follow the world. By our actions and our speech, the world sees that we are different. The way we stand proves that we've been captivated by God.

Grace is too precious a treasure to keep to ourselves. When we're transformed by the renewing of our minds, we get a clearer view of our incorruptible inheritance.

I pray you lay hold of the miracle-working power of grace in your life. God loves you. Allow Him to teach you the riches of His grace. You truly have been destined to know, to walk, and to minister His truth today.

LIFE FOUNDATIONS

CONTACT INFORMATION

Charis Bible College

800 Gospel Truth Way

Woodland Park, CO 80863

info@charisbiblecollege.org

Helpline Available 24/7: 719-635-1111

CharisBibleCollege.org

Also visit Carrie at: CarriePickett.com